In the Year 1963

By

Kerry Butters.

In the Year 1963

Millennium:	2nd millennium
Centuries:	19th century – **20th century** – 21st century
Decades:	1930s 1940s 1950s – **1960s** – 1970s 1980s 1990s
Years:	1960 1961 1962 – **1963** – 1964 1965 1966

1963 (MCMLXIII) was a common year starting on Tuesday (dominical letter F) of the Gregorian calendar, the 1963rd year of the Common Era (CE) and *Anno Domini* (AD) designations, the 963rd year of the 2nd millennium, the 63rd year of the 20th century, and the 4th year of the 1960s decade.

Contents

- 1 Events
- 2 Births
- 3 Deaths
- 4 Nobel Prizes
- 5 In the News

Events

January

- January 1
  - Osamu Tezuka's *Tetsuwan Atomu (Astro Boy)*, Japan's first serialized animated series based on the popular manga, debuts on Japanese television station Fuji Television.
  - Bogle–Chandler case: Commonwealth Scientific and Industrial Research Organisation scientist Dr. Gilbert Bogle and Mrs. Margaret Chandler are found dead (presumed poisoned), in bushland near the Lane Cove River, Sydney, Australia.

January 8: *Mona Lisa* in Washington, D.C.

- January 2 – Vietnam War: The Viet Cong win their first major victory in the Battle of Ap Bac.
- January 8 – Leonardo da Vinci's *Mona Lisa* is exhibited in the United States for the first time, at the National Gallery of Art in Washington, D.C.

- January 14
  - George Wallace becomes governor of Alabama. In his inaugural speech, he defiantly proclaims "segregation now, segregation tomorrow, and segregation forever!"
  - The steam locomotive *Flying Scotsman* (British Railways No. 60103) makes its last scheduled run, before going into the hands of Alan Pegler for preservation.
- January 18 – Due to severe winter conditions the twelfth *elfstedentocht* skating tour in the Netherlands turns into an almost total disaster. Of the 9,294 participants only 69 manage to finish, making this the heaviest *elfstedentocht* ever held.
- January 22 – France and West Germany sign the Élysée Treaty.
- January 26 – The Australia Day shootings rock Perth; 2 people are shot dead and 3 others injured by Eric Edgar Cooke.
- January 28 – Black student Harvey Gantt enters Clemson University in South Carolina, the last U.S. state to hold out against racial integration.
- January 29 – French President Charles de Gaulle vetoes the United Kingdom's entry into the European Common Market.

February

- February 5 – The European Court of Justice's ruling in *Van Gend en Loos v Nederlandse Administratie der Belastingen* establishes the principle of direct effect, one of the basic tenets of European Union law.
- February 8 – Travel, financial and commercial transactions by United States citizens to Cuba are made illegal by the John F. Kennedy Administration.
- February 10 – Five Japanese cities located on the northernmost part of Kyūshū are merged and become the city of Kitakyūshū, with a population of more than 1 million.
- February 11
  - The Central Intelligence Agency's Domestic Operations Division is created in the United States.

- The Beatles record their debut album *Please Please Me* in a single day at the Abbey Road Studios in London.
- American-born poet Sylvia Plath commits suicide in London.
- February 12 – Northwest Airlines Flight 705 crashes in the Florida Everglades, killing all 43 aboard.
- February 14 – Harold Wilson becomes leader of the opposition Labour Party in the United Kingdom; in October 1964 he became prime minister.
- February 19 – The publication of Betty Friedan's *The Feminine Mystique* launches the reawakening of the Women's Movement in the United States as women's organizations and consciousness raising groups spread.
- February 21 – An earthquake destroys the village of Marj, Libya, killing 900.
- February 27
  - Juan Bosch takes office as the 41st president of the Dominican Republic.
  - Female suffrage is enacted in Iran.
- February 28 – Dorothy Schiff resigns from the New York Newspaper Publishers' Association, feeling that the city needs at least one paper as New York's 83-day newspayer strike ensued. Her paper, the *New York Post*, resumes publication on March 4.

March

- March
  - The divorce case of The Duke and Duchess of Argyll causes scandal in the United Kingdom.

March 21: Alcatraz closes

- March 4 – In Paris, six people are sentenced to death for conspiring to assassinate President Charles de Gaulle. De Gaulle pardons five, but the other conspirator, Jean Bastien-Thiry, is executed by firing squad several days later.

- March 5 – In Camden, Tennessee, country music superstar Patsy Cline (Virginia Patterson Hensley) is killed in a plane crash along with fellow performers Hawkshaw Hawkins, Cowboy Copas and Cline's manager and pilot Randy Hughes, while returning from a benefit performance in Kansas City, Kansas, for country radio disc jockey "Cactus" Jack Call.
- March 17 – Mount Agung erupts on Bali, killing approximately 1,500.
- March 18 – *Gideon v. Wainwright*: The Supreme Court of the United States rules that state courts are required to provide counsel in criminal cases for defendants who cannot afford to pay their own attorneys.
- March 21 – The Alcatraz Federal Penitentiary on Alcatraz Island in San Francisco Bay closes; the last 27 prisoners are transferred elsewhere at the order of United States Attorney General Robert F. Kennedy.
- March 22 – The Beatles release their first album, *Please Please Me*, in the United Kingdom.
- March 23 – *Dansevise* by Grethe & Jørgen Ingmann (music by Otto Francker, text by Sejr Volmer-Sørensen) wins the Eurovision Song Contest 1963 for Denmark.

March 27: British Rail network, as it would have become, if "Beeching axe" plans had been fully implemented (only bolded rail lines would have remained).

- March 27 – In Britain, Dr. Richard Beeching issues a report, *The Reshaping of British Railways*, calling for huge cuts to the country's rail network.
- March 28 – Director Alfred Hitchcock's film *The Birds* is released in the United States.
- March 30 – Indigenous Australians are legally allowed to drink alcohol in New South Wales.
- March 31 – The 1962–63 New York City newspaper strike ends after 114 days.

April

- April 1 – The long-running soap opera *General Hospital* debuts on ABC Television in the United States.
- April 3 – Southern Christian Leadership Conference volunteers kick off the Birmingham campaign (Birmingham, Alabama) against racial segregation in the United States with a sit-in.
- April 7 – Yugoslavia is proclaimed to be a socialist republic, and Josip Broz Tito is named President for Life.
- April 8 – The 35th Academy Awards ceremony is held. *Lawrence of Arabia* wins Best Picture.
- April 9 – British statesman Sir Winston Churchill becomes an honorary citizen of the United States.
- April 10 – The U.S. nuclear submarine *Thresher* sinks 220 mi (190 nmi; 350 km) east of Cape Cod; all 129 aboard (112 crewmen plus yard personnel) die.
- April 12
  - Martin Luther King Jr., Ralph Abernathy, Fred Shuttlesworth and others are arrested in a Birmingham, Alabama protest for "parading without a permit".
  - The Soviet nuclear powered submarine *K-33* collides with the Finnish merchant vessel M/S *Finnclipper* in the Danish Straits. Although severely damaged, both vessels make it to port.
- April 14 – The Institute of Mental Health (Belgrade) is established.

- April 15 – 70,000 marchers arrive in London from Aldermaston, to demonstrate against nuclear weapons.
- April 16 – Martin Luther King, Jr. issues his "Letter from Birmingham Jail".
- April 20 – In Quebec, Canada, members of the terrorist group Front de libération du Québec bomb a Canadian Army recruitment center, killing night watchman Wilfred V. O'Neill.
- April 21–April 23 – The first election of the Supreme Institution of the Bahá'í Faith (known as the Universal House of Justice, whose seat is at the Bahá'í World Centre on Mount Carmel in Haifa, Israel) is held.
- April 22 – Lester Bowles Pearson becomes the 14th Prime Minister of Canada.
- April 28 – A general election is held in Italy.
- April 29 – Buddy Rogers becomes the first WWWF Champion.

May

- May 1 – The Coca-Cola Company introduces its first diet drink, Tab cola.
- May 2
  - Thousands of blacks, many of them children, are arrested while protesting segregation in Birmingham, Alabama. Public Safety Commissioner Eugene "Bull" Connor later unleashes fire hoses and police dogs on the demonstrators.
  - Berthold Seliger launches near Cuxhaven a 3-stage rocket with a maximum flight altitude of more than 62 miles (the only sounding rocket developed in Germany).
- May 4 – The Le Monde Theater fire in Dioirbel, Senegal kills 64.
- May 8
  - *Dr. No*, the first James Bond film, is shown in U.S. theaters.
  - Huế Phật Đản shootings: The Army of the Republic of Vietnam opens fire on Buddhists who defy a ban on the flying of the Buddhist flag on Vesak, the birthday of Gautama Buddha, killing 9. (Earlier, President Ngô Đình Diệm allowed the flying of the Vatican flag in honour of his

brother, Archbishop Ngô Đình Thục.) Start of Buddhist crisis in South Vietnam.
- CVS Pharmacy opens in Lowell, Massachusetts.
- May 12 – *The Shanty* is established in New Castle, Indiana
- May 13 – A smallpox outbreak hits Stockholm, Sweden, lasting until July.
- May 14 – Kuwait becomes the 111th member of the United Nations.
- May 15 – Project Mercury: NASA launches Gordon Cooper on Mercury-Atlas 9, the last mission (on June 12 NASA Administrator James E. Webb tells Congress the program is complete).
- May 22 – A.C. Milan beats Benfica 2-1 at Wembley Stadium, London and wins the 1962–63 European Cup (football).
- May 23 – Fidel Castro visits the Soviet Union.
- May 25 – The Organisation of African Unity is established in Addis Ababa, Ethiopia.
- May 27 – *The Freewheelin' Bob Dylan* is singer-songwriter Bob Dylan's second studio album, and most influential, opening with the song "Blowin' in the Wind", released by Columbia Records.

June

- June 3
  - Huế chemical attacks: The Army of the Republic of Vietnam rains liquid chemicals on the heads of Buddhist protestors, injuring 67 people. The United States threatens to cut off aid to the regime of Ngô Đình Diệm.
  - Pope John XXIII dies.
- June 4 – President John F. Kennedy signs Executive Order 11110, authorizing the Secretary of the Treasury to issue silver certificates.
- June 5 – The first annual National Hockey League Entry Draft is held in Montreal.
- June 10 – President John F. Kennedy delivers his American University speech, "A Strategy of Peace", in Washington, D.C.

- June 10 – The University of Central Florida is established by the Florida legislature.
- June 11
  - In Saigon, Buddhist monk Thích Quảng Đức commits self-immolation to protest the oppression of Buddhists by the Ngô Đình Diệm administration.
  - Alabama Governor George Wallace stands in the door of the University of Alabama to protest against integration, before stepping aside and allowing blacks James Hood and Vivian Malone to enroll.
  - President John F. Kennedy broadcasts a historic Civil Rights Address, in which he promises a Civil Rights Bill, and asks for "the kind of equality of treatment that we would want for ourselves".
- June 12
  - Medgar Evers is murdered in Jackson, Mississippi. (His killer, Byron De La Beckwith, is convicted in 1994.)
  - The film *Cleopatra* is released.
- June 13
  - The cancellation of Mercury-Atlas 10 effectively ends the United States' manned spaceflight Project Mercury.
  - The New York Commodity Exchange begins trading silver futures contracts.
- June 15 – The AC Cobra makes its first appearance at the 24 Hours of Le Mans. It would go on to win its class the following year.
- June 16 – *Vostok 6* carries Soviet cosmonaut Valentina Tereshkova, the first woman into space.
- June 17 – *Abington School District v. Schempp*: The U.S. Supreme Court rules that state-mandated Bible reading in public schools is unconstitutional.
- June 19 – Valentina Tereshkova the first woman in space, returns to Earth.
- June 20
  - Establishment of the Moscow–Washington hotline (officially, the Direct Communications Link or DCL; unofficially, the "red telephone"; and in fact a teleprinter

link) is authorized by signing of a Memorandum of Understanding in Geneva by representatives of the Soviet Union and the United States.
- o Swedish Air Force Colonel Stig Wennerström is arrested as a spy for the Soviet Union.
- June 21 – Pope Paul VI (Giovanni Battista Montini) succeeds Pope John XXIII as the 262nd pope.
- June 26 – John F. Kennedy gives his "Ich bin ein Berliner" speech in West Berlin, East Germany.
- June – UNESCO *History of Mankind*, vol. 1 published.

July

- July 1 – ZIP codes are introduced by the United States Postal Service.
- July 5
  - o Diplomatic relations between the Israeli and the Japanese governments are raised to embassy level.
- July 7 – Double Seven Day scuffle: Secret police loyal to Ngô Đình Nhu, brother of President Ngô Đình Diệm, attack American journalists including Peter Arnett and David Halberstam at a demonstration during the Buddhist crisis in South Vietnam.
- July 11 – South Africa: police raid Liliesleaf Farm to the north of Johannesburg, arresting a group of ANC leaders.
- July 12 – Pauline Reade (16) is abducted by Ian Brady and Myra Hindley in Manchester, England, the first victim of the Moors murders; her remains are located in July 1987.
- July 19 – American test pilot Joe Walker, flying the X-15, reaches an altitude of 65.8 miles (105.9 kilometers), making it a sub-orbital spaceflight by recognized international standards.
- July 26
  - o An earthquake in Skopje, Yugoslavia (present-day Republic of Macedonia) leaves 1,800 dead.
  - o NASA launches Syncom 2, the world's first geostationary (synchronous) satellite.

- July 30 – The Soviet newspaper *Izvestia* reports that British diplomat and double agent Kim Philby has been given asylum in Moscow.

August

August 28: March on Washington for Jobs and Freedom

- August 5 – The United States, United Kingdom, and Soviet Union sign the Partial Nuclear Test Ban Treaty.
- August 8 – The Great Train Robbery takes place in Buckinghamshire, England.
- August 15 – Trois Glorieuses: President Fulbert Youlou is overthrown in the Republic of Congo after a three-day uprising in the capital, Brazzaville.
- August 18 – American civil rights movement: James Meredith becomes the first black person to graduate from the University of Mississippi.
- August 21 – Xá Lợi Pagoda raids: The Army of the Republic of Vietnam Special Forces loyal to Ngô Đình Nhu, brother of President Ngô Đình Diệm, vandalise Buddhist pagodas across South Vietnam, arresting thousands and leaving an estimated hundreds dead. In the wake of the raids, the Kennedy administration by Cable 243 orders the United States Embassy, Saigon to explore alternative leadership in the country, opening the way towards a coup against Diệm.

- August 22 – American test pilot Joe Walker again achieves a sub-orbital spaceflight according to international standards, this time by piloting the X-15 to an altitude of 67.0 miles (107.8 kilometers).
- August 28 – Martin Luther King Jr. delivers his "I Have a Dream" speech on the steps of the Lincoln Memorial to an audience of at least 250,000, during the March on Washington for Jobs and Freedom.

September

- September 1 – The language border in Belgium is fixed. This will become the foundation for the further federalization of the county.
- September 5 – British prostitute Christine Keeler is arrested for perjury for her part in the Profumo affair. On December 6 she is sentenced to 9 months in prison.
- September 6 – The Centre for International Intellectual Property Studies (CEIPI) is founded.
- September 7 – The Pro Football Hall of Fame opens in Canton, Ohio with 17 charter members.
- September 10 – Mafia boss Bernardo Provenzano is indicted for murder (he is captured 43 years later, on April 11, 2006).
- September 15 – American civil rights movement: The 16th Street Baptist Church bombing, in Birmingham, Alabama, kills 4 and injures 22.
- September 16 – Malaysia is formed through the merging of the Federation of Malaya and the British crown colony of Singapore, North Borneo (renamed Sabah) and Sarawak.
- September 18 – Rioters burn down the British Embassy in Jakarta, to protest the formation of Malaysia.
- September 23 – King Fahd University of Petroleum and Minerals is established by a Saudi Royal Decree as the *College of Petroleum and Minerals*.
- September 24 – The United States Senate ratifies the Partial Nuclear Test Ban Treaty.

- September 25
  - The Denning Report on the Profumo affair is published in Great Britain.
  - In the Dominican Republic, Juan Bosch is deposed by a coup d'état led by the military with civilian support.
- September 29
  - The second period of the Second Vatican Council in Rome opens.
  - The University of East Anglia is established in Norwich, England.

October

- October 1
- October 2 John F. Kennedy Toasts of the President and Emperor Haile Selassie at a Luncheon in Rockville, Maryland.
  - Nigeria becomes a republic; The 1st Republican Constitution is established.
  - In the U.S., the President's Commission on the Status of Women issues its final reports to President Kennedy.
- October 3 – 1963 Honduran coup d'état: A violent coup in Honduras pre-empts the October 13 election, ends a period of reform under President Ramón Villeda Morales and begins two decades of military rule under General Oswaldo López Arellano.
- October 4 – Hurricane Flora, one of the worst Atlantic storms in history, hits Hispaniola and Cuba, killing nearly 7,000 people.
- October 8 – Sam Cooke and his band are arrested after trying to register at a "whites only" motel in Louisiana. In the months following, he records the song "A Change Is Gonna Come".
- October 9 – In northeast Italy, over 2,000 people are killed when a large landslide behind the Vajont Dam causes a giant wave of water to overtop it.
- October 10
  - The Partial Nuclear Test Ban Treaty, signed on August 5, takes effect.

- The second James Bond film, *From Russia with Love*, opens in the UK.
- October 14 – A revolution starts in Radfan, South Yemen, against British colonial rule.
- October 16 – The thousandth day of John F. Kennedy's presidency.
- October 19 – Alec Douglas-Home succeeds Harold Macmillan as Prime Minister of the United Kingdom.
- October 28 – Demolition of the 1910 Pennsylvania Station begins in New York City, continuing until 1966.
- October 30 – The car manufacturing firm Lamborghini is founded in Italy.
- October 31 – 74 die in a gas explosion during a Holiday on Ice show at the Indiana State Fair Coliseum in Indianapolis.

November

- November 1 – Arecibo Observatory, a radio telescope, officially begins operation in Puerto Rico.
- November 2 – 1963 South Vietnamese coup: Arrest and assassination of Ngo Dinh Diem, the South Vietnamese President.
- November 6 – 1963 South Vietnamese coup: Coup leader General Dương Văn Minh takes over as leader of South Vietnam.
- November 7 – 11 German miners are rescued from a collapsed mine after 14 days in what became known as the "Wunder von Lengede" ("miracle of Legend").
- November 8 – Finnair aircraft OH-LCA crashes before landing at Mariehamn Airport on the Åland Islands.
- November 9 – Two disasters in Japan:
  - Miike coal mine explosion: A coal mine explosion kills 458 and sends 839 carbon monoxide poisoning victims to hospital.
  - Tsurumi rail accident: A triple train disaster in Yokohama kills 161.
- November 10 – Malcolm X makes an historic speech in Detroit, Michigan ("Message to the Grass Roots").

- November 14 – A volcanic eruption under the sea near Iceland creates a new island, Surtsey.
- November 16 – A newspaper strike begins in Toledo, Ohio.
- November 18
    - The Dartford Tunnel opens in England.
    - The first push-button telephone is made available to AT&T customers.

November 22: Lyndon B. Johnson is sworn in as U.S. President after assassination of John F. Kennedy.

- November 22
    - Assassination of John F. Kennedy: In a motorcade in Dallas, Texas, U.S. President John F. Kennedy is fatally shot by Lee Harvey Oswald, and Governor of Texas John Connally is seriously wounded. Upon Kennedy's death, Vice President Lyndon B. Johnson becomes President of the United States. A few hours later, President Johnson is sworn in aboard Air Force One, as Kennedy's body is flown back to Washington, D.C. Stores and businesses shut down for the entire weekend and Monday, in tribute.
    - English-born writer Aldous Huxley, author of *Brave New World*, dies of cancer in the United States.
    - Irish-born theologian and writer C. S. Lewis, author of works including *The Chronicles of Narnia*, *The Screwtape Letters* and *Mere Christianity*, dies of renal failure at his home in Oxford (England).
    - Phil Spector's *A Christmas Gift for You from Phil Spector* is released.

- The Beatles' second UK album, *With the Beatles*, is released.
- November 23
  - Moors murders: John Kilbride (12) is abducted by Ian Brady and Myra Hindley in England.
  - The first episode of the BBC television series *Doctor Who* is broadcast in the United Kingdom.
  - The Golden Age Nursing Home fire kills 63 elderly people near Fitchville, Ohio.
- November 24
  - Lee Harvey Oswald, assassin of John F. Kennedy, is shot dead by Jack Ruby in Dallas, an event seen on live national television.
  - Vietnam War: New U.S. President Lyndon B. Johnson confirms that the United States intends to continue supporting South Vietnam militarily and economically.
- November 25 – State funeral of John F. Kennedy: President Kennedy is buried at Arlington National Cemetery. Schools around the nation cancel classes that day; millions watch the funeral on live international television.
- November 29
  - U.S. President Lyndon B. Johnson establishes the Warren Commission to investigate the assassination of John F. Kennedy.
  - Trans-Canada Air Lines Flight 831, a Douglas DC-8 crashes into a wooded hillside after taking-off from Dorval International Airport near Montreal, killing all 118 on board, the worst air disaster for many years in Canada's history.
  - Foundation stone for Mirzapur Cadet College is laid in East Pakistan (present-day Bangladesh).

December

- December 3 – The Warren Commission begins its investigation into the assassination of John F. Kennedy.
- December 4 – The second period of the Second Vatican Council closes.

- December 5 – The Seliger Forschungs-und-Entwicklungsgesellschaft mbH demonstrates rockets for military use to military representatives of non-NATO-countries near Cuxhaven. Although these rockets land via parachute at the end of their flight and no allied laws are violated, the Soviet Union protests this action.
- December 7 – Tony Verna, a CBS-TV director, debuts an improved version of instant replay during his direction of a live televised sporting event, the Army–Navy Game of college football played in Philadelphia. This instance is notable as it was the first instant replay system to use videotape instead of film.
- December 8
  - A lightning strike causes the crashing of Pan Am Flight 214 near Elkton, Maryland, killing 81 people.
  - Frank Sinatra, Jr. is kidnapped at Harrah's Lake Tahoe.
- December 10
  - In the United States, the X-20 Dyna-Soar spaceplane program is cancelled.
  - Chuck Yeager narrowly escapes death while testing an NF-104A rocket-augmented aerospace trainer when his aircraft goes out of control at 108,700 feet (nearly 21 miles up) and crashes. He parachutes to safety at 8,500 feet after vainly battling to gain control of the powerless, rapidly falling craft. In this incident he becomes the first pilot to make an emergency ejection in the full pressure suit needed for high altitude flights.
- December 12 – Kenya gains independence from the United Kingdom, with Jomo Kenyatta as prime minister.
- December 19 – Zanzibar gains independence from the United Kingdom, as a constitutional monarchy under Sultan Jamshid bin Abdullah.
- December 21 – Cyprus Emergency: Inter-communal fighting erupts between Greek and Turkish Cypriots.
- December 22 – The cruise ship *Lakonia* burns 180 miles (290 km) north of Madeira, with the loss of 128 lives.
-

- December 25
  - Walt Disney releases his 18th feature-length animated motion picture *The Sword in the Stone*, about the boyhood of King Arthur. It is the penultimate animated film personally supervised by Disney.
  - İsmet İnönü of the Republican People's Party (CHP) forms the new government of Turkey (28th government, coalition partners; independents, İnönü has served 10 ten times as a prime minister, this is his last government).
- December 26 – The Beatles' "I Want to Hold Your Hand" and "I Saw Her Standing There" are released in the United States, marking the beginning of Beatlemania on an international level.

Date unknown

- David H. Frisch and J.H. Smith prove that the radioactive decay of mesons is slowed by their motion (see Einstein's special relativity and general relativity).
- The Semi-Automatic Ground Environment for the defense of the United States is fully deployed.
- The TAT-3 transatlantic communications cable goes into operation.
- Ivan Sutherland writes the revolutionary Sketchpad program and runs it on the Lincoln TX-2 computer at Massachusetts Institute of Technology.
- Construction of Moscow's Ostankino Tower begins.
- The IEEE Computer Society is founded.
- The Urdu keyboard is standardised by the Central Language Board in Pakistan.
- Harvey Ball invents the ubiquitous smiley face symbol.
- The Reformed Druids of North America is founded.
- The 1955 film *Oklahoma!*, an adaptation of the famed Rodgers and Hammerstein musical, is re-released.
- The iconic Porsche 911 is first produced.
- Conference Premier football club Welling United is formed.

Births

January

José Mourinho

Till Lindemann

Dave Foley

- January 1 – Linda Henry, English actress
- January 2
  - David Cone, American baseball player
  - Edgar Martínez, American baseball player

- January 4
  - Till Lindemann, German singer (Rammstein)
  - Dave Foley, Canadian actor and comedian
- January 6 – Tony Halme, Finnish boxer and politician (d. 2010)
- January 7 – Rand Paul U.S Senator from Kentucky
- January 13 – Jiang Wen, Chinese actor
- January 14 – Steven Soderbergh, American film director
- January 15 – Mathias Döpfner, journalist and chief executive officer of German media group Axel Springer SE
- January 16 – James May, English motoring journalist and television show host
- January 18 – Ian Crook, English footballer
- January 17 – Kai Hansen, German power metal guitarist and singer
- January 19 – Caron Wheeler, British singer-songwriter (Soul II Soul)
- January 20 – Firebreaker Chip, American professional wrestler
- January 21
  - Hakeem Olajuwon, Nigerian basketball player
  - Detlef Schrempf, German basketball player
- January 23 – Gail O'Grady, American actress
- January 24 – Arnold Vanderlyde, Dutch boxer
- January 26
  - Chin Siu-ho, Hong Kong actor
  - Jazzie B, British DJ, music producer (Soul II Soul)
  - José Mourinho, Portuguese football manager
  - Andrew Ridgeley, English singer
- January 29 – Octave Octavian Teodorescu, Romanian composer, vanguard rock musician, multi-instrumentist
- January 30
  - Thomas Brezina, Austrian author
  - Shōko Tsuda, Japanese voice actress

February

Michael Jordan

Larry the Cable Guy

Seal

William Baldwin

- February 2 – Eva Cassidy, American vocalist (d. 1996)
- February 3 – Gretel Killeen, Australian journalist
- February 4 – Pirmin Zurbriggen, Swiss alpine skier
- February 8
  - Joshua Kadison, American singer-songwriter
  - Gene Steratore, American football official
- February 10 – Smiley Culture, British reggae singer (d. 2011)
- February 11 – Diane Franklin, American actress
- February 12 – Brent Jones, American football player
- February 14
  - Enrico Colantoni, Canadian actor
  - D'wayne Wiggins, American singer-songwriter and record producer (Tony! Toni! Toné!)
- February 17
  - Michael Jordan, American former professional basketball player
  - Larry the Cable Guy, American actor and comedian
- February 18 – Rob Andrew, English rugby union player
- February 19
  - Seal, English singer
  - Jessica Tuck, American actress
- February 20 – Charles Barkley, American basketball player
- February 21 – William Baldwin, American actor
- February 22
  - Vijay Singh, Fiji golfer
  - Don Wakamatsu, American baseball player
- February 23 – Bobby Bonilla, American baseball player
- February 26 – Chase Masterson, American actress and singer
- February 27 – Virginie Boutaud, Brazilian singer and actress (Metrô, Virginie & Fruto Proibido)

March

Quentin Tarantino

- March 1
    - Thomas Anders, German singer (Modern Talking)
    - Russell Wong, American actor
- March 2 – Tuff Hedeman, American PRCA World Champion Bull Rider
- March 3 – Martín Fiz, Spanish long-distance runner
- March 4
    - Jason Newsted, American bassist
    - Daniel Roebuck, American actor
- March 5
    - Thomas Hermanns, German TV-presenter, director, TV-author and comedian
    - Joel Osteen, American televangelist and son of John Osteen
- March 6 – Gary L. Stevens, American jockey
- March 7 – Kim Ung-yong, Korean child prodigy
- March 12 – Joaquim Cruz, Brazilian runner
- March 13 – Fito Páez, Argentine musician
- March 14
    - Bruce Reid, Australian cricketer
    - Mike Rochford, Major League Baseball pitcher
    - Andrew Fleming, American film director
    - Mahiro Maeda, Japanese animators
- March 15 – Bret Michaels, American rock singer (Poison)
- March 17 – Alex Fong, Hong Kong actor
-

- March 18
  - Jeff LaBar, American rock guitarist
  - Ratna Pathak, Indian film actress
  - Vanessa L. Williams, African-American beauty queen, actress, and singer
- March 19 – Mary Scheer, American actress and comedian
- March 20
  - Paul Annacone, American tennis player and coach
  - Kathy Ireland, American model and actress
  - David Thewlis, English actor
- March 21 – Ronald Koeman, Dutch football player and manager
- March 22 – Susan Ann Sulley, British musician
- March 23 – Jose Miguel Gonzalez Martin del Campo, Spanish football player
- March 24 – John T. Chisholm, American prosecutor; District Attorney of Milwaukee County, Wisconsin (2007–present)
- March 26 – Natsuhiko Kyogoku, Japanese writer
- March 27
  - Charly Alberti, Argentinian musician
  - Dave Koz, American jazz musician
  - Quentin Tarantino, American actor, director, writer, and producer
  - Xuxa, Brazilian television personality
- March 28 – Chieko Honda, Japanese voice actress (d. 2013)

April

Graham Norton

Rafael Correa

Garry Kasparov

Conan O'Brien

Jet Li

- April 3
  - Karl Beattie, British director, husband of Yvette Fielding
  - Criss Oliva, American metal guitarist (Savatage) (d. 1993)
- April 4
  - Jack Del Rio, American football player and coach
  - Dale Hawerchuk, Canadian ice hockey player
  - Graham Norton, Irish comedian and talk show host
  - Frank Yallop, Canadian footballer
- April 6 – Rafael Correa, President of Ecuador
- April 8 – Julian Lennon, British musician, son of John Lennon
- April 9 – Joe Scarborough, American newscaster
- April 10
  - Warren DeMartini, American rock guitarist
  - Doris Leuthard, Swiss politician and lawyer
  - Dean Norris, American actor
- April 11 – Chris Ferguson, American poker player
- April 12
  - Michael English, American Christian musician
  - Ai Orikasa, Japanese voice actress and singer
- April 13 – Garry Kasparov, Russian chess player
- April 15 – Beata Szydło, Prime Minister of Poland
- April 16 – Jimmy Osmond, American singer
- April 17 – Joel Murray, American actor
- April 18
  - Eric McCormack, Canadian actor
  - Conan O'Brien, American television entertainer and talk show host
- April 19 – Valerie Plame, former United States CIA Operations officer
- April 21
  - Ken Caminiti, American baseball player (d. 2004)
  - Roy Dupuis, Canadian actor
- April 24 – Tõnu Trubetsky, Estonian rock musician (Vennaskond)
- April 25 – Pascal of Bollywood, French singer
- April 26
  - Jet Li, Chinese martial artist and actor

- o Colin Scotts, Australian-born American football player
- April 27
  - o Russell T. Davies, Welsh television producer and writer
  - o Cali Timmins, Canadian actress
- April 29 – Mike Babcock, Canadian ice hockey coach
- April 30 – Michael Waltrip, American race car driver

May

Mike Myers

Viktor Orbán

- May 1 – Benjamin LaGuer, American prisoner proclaiming innocence for more than two decades
- May 2 – Ray Traylor, American professional wrestler ("Big Boss Man") (d. 2004)
- May 5 – James LaBrie, Canadian vocalist (Dream Theater)
- May 9 – Gary Daniels, British martial artist and actor
- May 10 – A. Raja, Indian politician
- May 11 – Natasha Richardson, English actress (d. 2009)
- May 12 – Jerry Trimble, American actor and martial artist

- May 16
  - Jon Coffelt, American artist
  - Mercedes Echerer, Austrian actress and politician
- May 23 – Wally Dallenbach Jr., American race car driver and announcer
- May 24
  - Michael Chabon, American author
  - Joe Dumars, American basketball player
  - Rich Rodriguez, American football coach
- May 25
  - Mike Myers, Canadian actor and comedian
  - Eha Rünne, Estonian shot putter and discus thrower
- May 26 – Clive Cowdery, English insurance entrepreneur
- May 29 – Lisa Whelchel, American actress, singer and writer
  - Tracey E. Bregman, American actress and designer
- May 31
  - Viktor Orbán, Prime Minister of Hungary
  - Wesley Willis, American outsider musician (d. 2003)

June

Johnny Depp

Helen Hunt

George Michael

- June 1 – David Westhead, English actor and producer
- June 4 – Sean Fitzpatrick, New Zealand rugby union player
- June 5 – Joe Rudán, Hungarian heavy metal singer
- June 6 – Jason Isaacs, British actor
- June 9 – Johnny Depp, American actor
- June 12
  - Warwick Capper, Australian rules footballer
  - Tim DeKay, American character actor
  - Jerry Lynn, American professional wrestler
- June 13 – Bettina Bunge, German tennis player
- June 14 – Rambo Amadeus, Montenegrin singer-songwriter
- June 15 – Helen Hunt, American actress
- June 16 – The Sandman, American professional wrestler
- June 17 – Greg Kinnear, American actor
- June 18
  - Bruce Smith, American football player
  - Juan Chioran, Argentine-Canadian actor
- June 20 – Amir Derakh, American musician

- June 22
  - Randy Couture, American mixed martial arts fighter
  - John Tenta, Canadian wrestler (d. 2006)
- June 23 – Colin Montgomerie, Scottish golfer
- June 24
  - Preki, Serbia-born American footballer
  - Mike Wieringo, American comic-book artist (d. 2007)
- June 25
  - Doug Gilmour, Canadian hockey player
  - Yann Martel, Canadian author
  - George Michael, English singer
- June 26 – Mikhail Khodorkovsky, Russian businessman, activist and former oligarch
- June 29 – Anne-Sophie Mutter, German violinist
- June 30 – Yngwie Malmsteen, Swedish guitarist, composer, and bandleader

July

Phoebe Cates

King Letsie III

Matti Nykänen

Lisa Kudrow

- July 4 – Christopher G. Kennedy, son of Attorney General Robert F. Kennedy
- July 6 – Miguel Garikoitz Aspiazu Rubina, Basque separatist
- July 11 – Lisa Rinna, American actress
- July 13 – Spud Webb, American basketball player
- July 15 – Brigitte Nielsen, Danish actress
- July 16 – Phoebe Cates, American actress
- July 17
  - King Letsie III of Lesotho
  - Suha Arafat, widow of Yasser Arafat
  - Matti Nykänen, Finnish ski jumper
- July 18
  - Martín Torrijos, President of Panama
  - Al Snow, American professional wrestler
- July 22 – Emilio Butragueño, Spanish football player
-

- July 24
  - Julie Krone, American jockey
  - Karl Malone, American basketball player
- July 27 – Donnie Yen, Hong Kong actor and martial artist
- July 28 – Beverley Craven, British singer-songwriter
- July 29
  - Jim Beglin, Irish football commentator
  - Graham Poll, English football referee
- July 30
  - Lisa Kudrow, American actress
  - Chris Mullin, American basketball player and executive

August

Sridevi

James Hetfield

Miro Cerar

- August 1 – Coolio, African-American rapper
- August 2 – Laura Bennett, American fashion designer
- August 3
  - Tasmin Archer, English singer
  - James Hetfield, American musician (Metallica)
- August 6 – Kevin Mitnick, American computer hacker
- August 7
  - Hiroaki Hirata, Japanese voice actor
  - Harold Perrineau, American actor
  - Wendy van der Plank, Welsh actress
- August 8
  - Rica Fukami, Japanese voice actress
  - Emi Shinohara, Japanese voice actress
  - Stephen Walkom, Canadian ice hockey official and executive
- August 9 – Whitney Houston, African-American singer (d. 2012)
- August 10 – Andrew Sullivan, British-born American blogger and political commentator
- August 13
  - Sridevi, Indian actress
  - Steve Higgins, American writer, producer, announcer, actor, and comedian
- August 15
  - Alejandro González Iñárritu, Mexican film director, producer and screenwriter

- o Valery Levaneuski, entrepreneur, politician, former political prisoner
- o August 16 – Christine Cavanaugh, American voice actress (d. 2014)
- August 17 – James Whitbourn, British composer
- August 18 – Heino Ferch, German actor
- August 19
  - o John Stamos, American actor
  - o Joey Tempest, Swedish singer-songwriter (Europe)
- August 22 – Tori Amos, American singer
- August 23
  - o Hans-Henning Fastrich, German field hockey player
  - o Park Chan-wook, South Korean film director and screenwriter
  - o Kenny Wallace, American race car driver
- August 24 – Hideo Kojima, Japanese video-game director
- August 25 – Miro Cerar, Prime Minister of Slovenia
- August 26
  - o Liu Huan, Chinese singer
  - o Michael Tao, Hong Kong actor
- August 30
  - o Michael Chiklis, American actor
  - o Phil Mills, British race car driver
- August 31
  - o Todd Carty, Irish actor
  - o Egyptian Lover, African-American rapper, DJ and producer

September

- September 1 – Carola Smit, Dutch musician
- September 6 – Geert Wilders, Dutch politician
- September 7 – Eric Wright (Eazy-E), African-American rapper (d. 1995)
- September 8 – Li Ning, Chinese gymnast
- September 9 – Markus Wasmeier, German alpine-skier
- September 10 – Randy Johnson, American baseball player

- September 11 – Joey Dedio, American actor
- September 12 – Norberto Barba, American cinematographer and film director
- September 14 – Robert Herjavec, Canadian businessman, investor, and television personality
- September 15 – Stephen C. Spiteri, Maltese military historian
- September 16 – Richard Marx, American pop/rock singer
- September 17 – Masahiro Chono, Japanese professional wrestler
- September 19
  - Jarvis Cocker, English rock musician (Pulp)
  - David Seaman, English football goalkeeper
- September 21
  - Cecil Fielder, American baseball player
  - Angus Macfadyen, Scottish actor
  - Mamoru Samuragochi, Japanese impostor
- September 28
  - Steve Blackman, American professional wrestler
  - Elliot Levine, Jazz musician and keyboardist with Heatwave (band)
- September 29
  - Dave Andreychuk, Canadian hockey player
  - Les Claypool, American bassist (Primus)

October

Elisabeth Shue

Lauren Holly

Rob Schneider

Farin Urlaub

- October 1 – Mark McGwire, American baseball player
- October 5
  - Dame Laura Davies, English golfer
  - Ronni Le Tekrø, Norwegian guitarist (TNT)
- October 6 – Elisabeth Shue, American actress
- October 10
  - Anita Mui, Hong Kong singer (d. 2003)

- o Daniel Pearl, American journalist (d. 2002)
- o Jolanda de Rover, Dutch swimmer
- October 12
  - o Satoshi Kon, Japanese anime director (d. 2010)
  - o Dave Legeno, English actor and mixed martial artist (d. 2014)
  - o Lane Frost, American rodeo champion (d. 1989)
- October 13
  - o Mabi de Almeida, Angolan professional football coach
- October 14
  - o Lori Petty, American actress, director, and screenwriter
  - o Alan McDonald, Northern Irish footballer
- October 17 – Norm Macdonald, Canadian comedian
- October 19 – Sinitta, Anglo-US singer
- October 20 – John Storgårds, Finnish conductor and violinist
- October 22 – Brian Boitano, American figure skater
- October 23
  - o Thomas Di Leva, Swedish singer
  - o Wilson Yip, Hong Kong actor and director
- October 25 – John Levén, Swedish bassist (Europe)
- October 26
  - o Natalie Merchant, American singer, songwriter, and musician
  - o Ted Demme, American director and producer (d. 2002)
- October 27
  - o Johnny Adair, Northern Irish/Ulster loyalist
  - o Feyyaz Uçar, Turkish footballer
  - o Farin Urlaub, German singer, band Die Ärzte
- October 28 – Lauren Holly, American actress
- October 30 – Kristina Wagner, American actress
- October 31
  - o Sarah Brown, wife of British Prime Minister Gordon Brown
  - o Johnny Marr, English musician
  - o Fred McGriff, American baseball player
  - o Dermot Mulroney, American actor
  - o Rob Schneider, American actor

November

Nicollette Sheridan

- November 1
    - Rick Allen, British rock musician (Def Leppard)
    - Mark Hughes, Welsh football player & manager
    - Katja Riemann, German actress
- November 2
    - Bobby Dall, American rock bassist (Poison)
    - Craig Saavedra, American filmmaker
- November 4 – Lena Zavaroni, Scottish entertainer (d. 1999)
- November 7 – John Barnes, Jamaican-born English footballer
- November 10 – Hugh Bonneville, British actor
- November 11 – Kip James, American professional wrestler
- November 13 – Vinny Testaverde, American football player
- November 15 – Benny Elias, Australian rugby player
- November 18 – Dante Bichette, American baseball player
- November 19
    - Terry Farrell, American actress
    - Jon Potter, British field hockey player
    - Peter Schmeichel, Danish football player
- November 21 – Nicollette Sheridan, English actress
- November 22 – Winsor Harmon, American actor
- November 23
    - Troy Hurtubise, Canadian inventor
    - Yoshino Takamori, Japanese voice actress
- November 25
    - Holly Cole, Canadian jazz singer

- Bernie Kosar, American football player

December

Benjamin Bratt

Brad Pitt

Jennifer Beals

Til Schweiger

Lars Ulrich

- December 2 – Ann Patchett, American novelist
- December 3 – Terri Schiavo, American right-to-die cause célèbre (d. 2005)
- December 4 – Sergey Bubka, Ukrainian pole vaulter
- December 7
  - Mark Bowen, Welsh footballer
  - Paul Dobson, British voice actor
- December 8
  - Greg Howe, American guitarist
  - Toshiaki Kawada, Japanese professional wrestler
- December 12
  - Juan Carlos Varela, President of Panama
  - Ai Orikasa, Japanese voice actress
- December 13
  - Uwe-Jens Mey, German speed skater
  - Jake White, South African rugby coach
- December 14
  - Cynthia Gibb, American actress
  - Vytautas Juozapaitis, Lithuanian baritone, professor and television host

- December 16
  - Benjamin Bratt, American actor
  - Jeff Carson, American singer
  - Bärbel Schäfer, German television presenter and talk show host
- December 18
  - Pauline Ester, French singer
  - Rikiya Koyama, Japanese voice actor
  - Charles Oakley, American basketball player
  - Brad Pitt, American actor
- December 19
  - Jennifer Beals, American actress
  - Til Schweiger, German actor
- December 21
  - Govinda Ahuja, Indian actor and politician
  - Jacques Simonet, Belgian politician (d. 2007)
- December 22
  - Vladimir Flórez, Colombian cartoonist
  - Bryan Gunn, Scottish footballer
  - Russell Lewis, British television writer and former child actor
  - Luna H. Mitani, Japanese-American Surrealist painter
- December 23
  - Jim Harbaugh, American football player and coach
  - Donna Tartt, American author
- December 24 – Sanjay Mehrotra, Indian entrepreneur
- December 26 – Lars Ulrich, Danish-born rock drummer (Metallica)
- December 29
  - Francisco Bustamante, Filipino billiard player
  - Sean Payton, American football coach
- December 30 – Kim Hill, American Christian singer

Date unknown

- Wei Brian, Chinese entrepreneur
- Gregory Henriquez, Canadian architect

Deaths

January

Sylvanus Olympio

Robert Frost

- January 1
    - Filippo Del Giudice, Italian film producer (b. 1892)
    - Robert S. Kerr, American businessman and politician (b. 1896)
- January 2
    - Jack Carson, Canadian actor (b. 1910)
    - Al Mamaux, professional baseball player and manager (b. 1894)
    - Dick Powell, American actor (b. 1904)

- January 5
  - Rogers Hornsby, American baseball player, (St. Louis Cardinals) and a member of the MLB Hall of Fame (b. 1896)
  - Erik Strandmark, Swedish film actor (b. 1919)
- January 6
  - Frank Tuttle, American film director (b. 1892)
  - Stark Young, American teacher, playwright, novelist, painter, literary critic, and essayist (b. 1881)
- January 7 – Erik Lundqvist, Swedish athlete (b. 1908)
- January 8
  - Boris Morros, American movie producer and FBI double agent (b. 1891)
  - Jack Okey, American art director (b. 1889)
- January 10 – Franz Planer, European film cinematographer (b. 1894)
- January 11 – Arthur Nock, English classicist, theologian, and Harvard University professor (b. 1902)
- January 13
  - Sonny Clark, American jazz pianist (b. 1931)
  - Sylvanus Olympio, 1st President of Togo (b. 1902)
- January 14 – Gustav Regler, German Socialist novelist (b. 1898)
- January 16
  - Cesare Fantoni, Italian film actor (b. 1905)
  - Gilardo Gilardi, Argentine composer, pianist, and conductor (b. 1889)
  - Mario Ruspoli, 2nd Prince of Poggio Suasa (b. 1867)
- January 18 – Edward Charles Titchmarsh, British mathematician (b. 1899)
- January 21 – Al St. John, American actor (b. 1893)
- January 23 – Józef Gosławski, Polish sculptor and medallic artist (b. 1908)
- January 24
  - Otto Harbach, American lyricist and librettist (b. 1873)
  - Kenneth Western, part of The Western Brothers (b. 1899)
- January 25 – Marion Sunshine, American actress (b. 1894)
- January 26 – Ole Olsen, American actor (b. 1892)

- January 27 – Evelyn Francisco, silent film actress (b. 1904)
- January 28
  - John Farrow, American film director (b. 1904)
  - Jean Piccard, Swiss-born chemist and engineer (b. 1884)
- January 29
  - Anthony Coldeway, American screenwriter (b. 1887)
  - Robert Frost, American poet, heart failure (b. 1874)
  - Lee Meadows, professional baseball player (b. 1894)
- January 30
  - Jane Gail, American silent movie and stage actress (b. 1890)
  - Cecil McGivern, British broadcasting executive and writer (b. 1907)
  - Francis Poulenc, French composer (b. 1899)
- January 31
  - Alasgar Alakbarov, Azerbaijani actor (b. 1910)
  - Ossie Vitt, professional baseball player and manager (b. 1890)

February

Abd al-Karim Qasim

- February 1
  - Louis D. Lighton, American screenwriter and producer (b. 1895)
  - Wyndham Standing, English actor (b. 1880)

- February 2 – William Gaxton, star of vaudeville, film, and theatre (b. 1893)
- February 6 – Piero Manzoni, Italian artist (b. 1933)
- February 8 – George Dolenz, American actor (b. 1908)
- February 9 – Abd al-Karim Qasim, Prime minister of Iraq (b. 1914)
- February 11 – Sylvia Plath, American poet and novelist (b. 1932)
- February 15
  - Edgardo Donato, Uruguayan tango composer and orchestra leader (b. 1897)
  - Louis J. Gasnier, French film director (b. 1875)
  - Bump Hadley, Major League Baseball pitcher (b. 1904)
- February 16
  - Else Jarlbak, Danish film actress (b. 1911)
  - László Lajtha, Hungarian composer, ethnomusicologist and conductor (b. 1892)
- February 18
  - Monte Blue, American actor (b. 1887)
  - Beppe Fenoglio, Italian writer (b. 1887)
  - Tokugawa Iemasa, Japanese politician, 17th head of the former Tokugawa shogunate (b. 1884)
- February 19 – Benny Moré, Cuban singer (b. 1919)
- February 20
  - Ferenc Fricsay, Hungarian conductor (b. 1914)
  - Jacob Gade, Danish violinist and composer (b. 1879)
  - Bill Hinchman, professional baseball player (b. 1883)
- February 22 – Arthur Guy Empey, soldier, author, screenwriter, and actor (b. 1883)
- February 24 – Herbert Asbury, American journalist and writer (b. 1889)
- February 28
  - Rajendra Prasad, Indian politician, 1st President of India (b. 1884)
  - Eppa Rixey, American baseball player (Cincinnati Reds) and a member of the MLB Hall of Fame (b. 1891)

March

- March 1 – Irish Meusel, American professional baseball player (b. 1893)
- March 4 – William Carlos Williams, American writer (b. 1883)
- March 5
  - Patsy Cline, American singer plane crash (b. 1932)
  - Cowboy Copas, American country music singer plane crash (b. 1913)
  - Ludde Gentzel, Swedish film actor (b. 1885)
  - Hawkshaw Hawkins, American country music singer plane crash (b. 1921)
  - Cyril Smith, Scottish actor heart attack (b. 1892)
- March 6 – Robert E. Cornish, scientist (b. 1903)
- March 7 – Joachim Holst-Jensen, Norwegian film actor (b. 1880)
- March 11
  - Ignat Bednarik, Romanian painter (b. 1882)
  - Joe Judge, American professional baseball player (b. 1894)
- March 16 – Archduchess Elisabeth Marie of Austria (b. 1883)
- March 17
  - Thomas Lennon, screenwriter (b. 1896)
  - Lizzie Miles, African American blues singer (b. 1895)
- March 18
  - Hubert Gough, British general (b. 1870)
  - Wanda Hawley, American actress (b. 1895)
- March 21 – Felice Minotti, Italian film actor (b. 1887)
- March 22
  - Cilly Aussem, German tennis champion (b. 1909)
  - Abraham Ellstein, American composer for Yiddish entertainments (b. 1907)
  - Mihály Székely, Hungarian bass singer (b. 1901)
- March 23 – Thoralf Skolem, Norwegian mathematician (b. 1887)
- March 25 – Felix Adler, American screenwriter (b. 1884)
- March 26 – Jean Bruce, French writer (b. 1921)
- March 27 – Harry Piel, German actor, film director, screenwriter, and film producer (b. 1892)

- March 28
    - Antoine Balpêtré, French film actor (b. 1898)
    - Frank J. Marion, American motion picture pioneer (b. 1869)
    - Alec Templeton, Welsh composer, pianist and satirist
- March 29
    - Pola Gojawiczyńska, Polish writer (b. 1896)
    - Wilcy Moore, American professional baseball player (b. 1897)
- March 31 – Harry Akst, American songwriter (b. 1894)

April

Alma Richards

Felix Manalo

- April 1 – Agnes Mowinckel, Norwegian actress and stage producer (b. 1875)

- April 3 – Alma Richards, American Olympic gold medalist (b. 1890)
- April 4
  - Jason Robards, Sr., American stage and screen actor, heart attack (b. 1892)
  - Oskari Tokoi, leader of the Social Democratic Party of Finland (b. 1873)
- April 6
  - Mario Fabrizi, comedian and actor, stress-related illness (b. 1924)
  - Otto Struve, Russian–American astronomer (b. 1897)
- April 7 – Amedeo Maiuri, Neapolitan archaeologist (b. 1886)
- April 9
  - Eddie Edwards, American jazz trombonist (b. 1891)
  - Benno Moiseiwitsch, Jewish-Ukrainian pianist (b. 1890)
  - Xul Solar, Argentine painter, sculptor, writer (b. 1887)
- April 11 – Nando Bruno, Italian film actor (b. 1895)
- April 12
  - Felix Manalo, First Executive Minister, Iglesia ni Cristo (b. 1886)
  - Herbie Nichols, American jazz pianist and composer (b. 1919)
- April 14
  - Arthur Jonath, German Olympic athlete (b. 1909)
  - Kodō Nomura, Japanese novelist and music critic (b. 1882)
  - Mahapandit Rahul Sankrityayan, Indian historian, writer, and scholar (b. 1893)
- April 15 – Edward Hearn, American actor (b. 1888)
- April 23
  - Ferruccio Cerio, Italian film writer and director (b. 1904)
  - Paul Fejos, Hungarian film director (b. 1897)
  - Harry Harper, professional baseball player (b. 1895)
  - Don C. Harvey, American television and film actor, cardiac arrest (b. 1911)
  - Frederick Peters, American film actor (b. 1884)
  -

- April 24
  - Rino Corso Fougier, Italian air force general (b. 1894)
  - Leonid Lukov, Soviet film director and screenwriter (b. 1909)
- April 25 – Christopher Hassall, English actor, dramatist, librettist, lyricist, and poet (b. 1912)
- April 26 – Roland Pertwee, English playwright, screenwriter, director, and actor (b. 1885)
- April 27 – Kenneth Macgowan, American film producer (b. 1888)
- April 30
  - Giovanni Grasso, Italian film actor (b. 1888)
  - William C. Mellor, American cinematographer, heart attack (b. 1903)
  - Bryant Washburn, American film actor, heart attack (b. 1889)

May

Robert Kerr

Mehdi Frasheri

- May 1 – Lope K. Santos, Filipino writer, Father of Philippine National Language and Grammar (b. 1879)
- May 2 – Van Wyck Brooks, American literary critic and writer (b. 1886)
- May 6 – Monty Woolley, American actor (b. 1888)
- May 7
  - Theodore von Kármán, Hungarian-American engineer and physicist (b. 1881)
  - Max Miller, British music hall performer (b. 1894)
- May 11 – Herbert Spencer Gasser, American physiologist, Nobel Prize laureate (b. 1888)
- May 12
  - Robert Kerr, Canadian sprinter (b. 1882)
  - A. W. Tozer, American Protestant pastor (b. 1897)
- May 18 – Ernie Davis, American football player, first African-American to win the Heisman Trophy (b. 1939)
- May 24 – Elmore James, American blues guitarist (b. 1918)
- May 25 – Mehdi Frashëri, Albanian politician, former Prime Minister (b. 1872)
- May 29 – Netta Muskett, British novelist (b. 1887)
- May 31 – Edith Hamilton, German-born author (b. 1867)

June

Pope John XXIII

Maria Guadalupe Garcia Zavala

- June 1 – Alfred V. Kidder, American archaeologist (b. 1885)
- June 3
  - Pope John XXIII (b. 1881)
  - Nâzım Hikmet, Turkish poet (b. 1902)
- June 7 – ZaSu Pitts, American actress (b. 1894)
- June 9 – Jacques Villon, French painter (b. 1875)
- June 10 – Anita King, American actress and race-car driver (b. 1884)
- June 11
  - Thích Quảng Đức, Vietnamese Buddhist monk (suicide) (b. 1897)
  - Syed Abdul Rahim, First Indian national football manager (b. 1909)
- June 12 – Medgar Evers, African-American civil rights activist (b. 1925)
- June 17
  - Robert James Hudson, Governor of Southern Rhodesia (b. 1885)
  - John Cowper Powys, novelist (b. 1872)
- June 18 – Pedro Armendáriz, Mexican actor (b. 1912)
- June 24 – Maria Guadalupe Garcia Zavala, Mexican saint (b. 1878)
- June 27 – John Maurice Clark, American economist (b. 1884)
- June 28 – Frank Baker, American baseball player (Philadelphia Athletics) and a member of the MLB Hall of Fame (b. 1886)

July

- July 6 – George, Duke of Mecklenburg, head of the House of Mecklenburg-Strelitz (b. 1899)
- July 10 – Teddy Wakelam, English sports broadcaster and rugby union player (b. 1893)
- July 12 – Slatan Dudow, Bulgarian film director (b. 1903)
- July 18 – Jack Solomon, American restaurateur (b. 1896)

August

- August 1 – Theodore Roethke, American poet (b. 1908)
- August 2 – Oliver La Farge, American writer (b. 1901)
- August 4 – Tom Keene, American actor (b. 1896)
- August 9 – Patrick Bouvier Kennedy, American infant son of President and Mrs. Kennedy
- August 10
  - Estes Kefauver, American politician (b. 1903)
  - Ernst Wetter, Swiss Federal Councillor (b. 1877)
- August 11 – Clem Bevans, American actor (b. 1879)
- August 17 – Richard Barthelmess, American actor (b. 1895)
- August 18 – Clifford Odets, American playwright (b. 1906)
- August 20 – Joan Voûte, Dutch astronomer (b. 1879)
- August 22 – William Morris, 1st Viscount Nuffield, British businessman and a philanthropist (b. 1877)
- August 23 – Larry Keating, American actor (b. 1896)
- August 24 – James Kirkwood, Sr., American film director (b. 1875)
- August 27
  - W. E. B. Du Bois, American civil rights activist (b. 1868)
  - Inayatullah Khan Mashriqi, Indian founder of the Khaksar Movement (b. 1888)
- August 30 – Guy Burgess, British spy, one of the Cambridge Five (b. 1911)
- August 31 – Georges Braque, French painter (b. 1882)

September

- September 3 – Louis MacNeice, Irish poet (b. 1907)
- September 4 – Robert Schuman, French statesman, a founding father of the European Union (b. 1886)
- September 11 – Suzanne Duchamp, French painter (b. 1889)
- September 12 – Modest Altschuler, Belarus-born American composer (b. 1873)
- September 17 – Eduard Spranger, German philosopher and psychologist (b. 1882)
- September 19 – David Low, New Zealand cartoonist (b. 1891)
- September 25
  - Alexander Sakharoff, Russian dancer and choreographer (b. 1886)
  - Kurt Zeitzler, German Army officer (b. 1895)

October

Édith Piaf

- October 4 – Lloyd Fredendall, American general (b. 1883)
- October 7 – Gustaf Gründgens, German actor (b. 1899)
- October 11
  - Jean Cocteau, French writer (b. 1889)
  - Édith Piaf, French singer and actress (b. 1915)
- October 15 – Alan Goodrich Kirk, American admiral (b. 1888)
- October 21 – Jean Decoux, French admiral, Governor-General of French Indochina (1940-1945) (b. 1884)
-

- October 24
  - Karl Bühler, German psychologist and linguist (b. 1879)
  - Beverly Wills, American actress (b. 1933)
- October 25 – Roger Désormière, French conductor (b. 1898)
- October 29 – Adolphe Menjou, American actor (b. 1890)
- October 31 – Henry Daniell, English actor (b. 1894)

November

Ngo Dinh Diem

- November 1
  - Elsa Maxwell, American gossip columnist (b. 1883)
  - Lê Quang Tung, South Vietnamese military leader (assassinated) (b. 1923)
- November 2
  - Ngô Đình Diệm, President of South Vietnam (assassinated) (b. 1901)
  - Ngô Đình Nhu, South Vietnamese military leader (assassinated) (b. 1910)
- November 12
  - José María Gatica, Argentine boxer (b. 1925)
  - John R. Hodge, United States Army general (b. 1893)
- November 15 – Fritz Reiner, Hungarian conductor (b. 1888)
- November 16 – Albert H. Pearson, American politician (b. 1920)
- November 21 – Robert Stroud, American prisoner, known as the "Birdman of Alcatraz" (b. 1890)
-

- November 22
  - Wilhelm Beiglböck, German Nazi physician at Dachau concentration camp (b. 1905)
  - Aldous Huxley, British writer (*Brave New World*) (b. 1894)
  - John F. Kennedy, 35th President of the United States (assassinated) (b. 1917)
  - C. S. Lewis, Irish-born British critic, novelist (*The Chronicles of Narnia*) and Christian apologist (b. 1898)
  - J. D. Tippit, American police officer with the Dallas Police Department (b. 1924)
- November 24 – Lee Harvey Oswald, American assassin of President John F. Kennedy (assassinated) (b. 1939)
- November 26 – Amelita Galli-Curci, Italian opera singer (b. 1882)
- November 28 – Ernesto Lecuona, Cuban composer (b. 1896)
- November 30 – Phil Baker, American comedian and radio personality (b. 1896)

December

Theodor Heuss

Paul Hindemith

- December – Andy Kennedy, Northern Ireland footballer (b. 1897)

- December 2
  - Sabu Dastagir, Indian-American actor (b. 1924)
  - Thomas Hicks, American runner (b. 1875)
- December 5 – Karl Amadeus Hartmann, German composer (b. 1905)
- December 10 – K. M. Panikkar, Indian scholar, diplomat and journalist (b. 1894)
- December 12
  - Theodor Heuss, 5th President of Germany (b. 1884)
  - Yasujirō Ozu, Japanese filmmaker (b. 1903)
- December 14 – Hubert Pierlot, former Prime Minister of Belgium (b. 1883)
- December 14 – Dinah Washington, African-American jazz/blues singer (b. 1924)
- December 15 – Rikidōzan, Korean-born Japanese professional wrestler (b. 1924)
- December 21 – Jack Hobbs, English cricketer (b. 1882)
- December 25 – Tristan Tzara, French poet (b. 1896)
- December 26 – Gorgeous George, American professional wrestler (b. 1915)
- December 28
  - Paul Hindemith, German composer (b. 1895)
  - A. J. Liebling, American journalist (b. 1904)

Nobel Prizes

- Physics – Eugene Wigner, Maria Goeppert-Mayer, and J. Hans D. Jensen
- Chemistry – Karl Ziegler and Giulio Natta
- Physiology or Medicine – Sir John Carew Eccles, Alan Lloyd Hodgkin, and Andrew Huxley
- Literature – Giorgos Seferis
- Peace – International Committee of the Red Cross, League of Red Cross Societies

In the News

The Soviet Union launches the Vostok 6 spacecraft, carrying Valentina Tereshkova, the first woman in space.

A hurricane and resulting Tsunami cause Flooding in East Pakistan Bangladesh kills 22,000.

The Profumo Crisis in the UK causing resignations from the cabinet caused by war minister John Profumo having an affair with Christina Wheeler who was also involved with a Soviet Navy officer.

NASA's final Project Mercury mission carrying astronaut Gordon Cooper launches from Cape Canaveral.

American Express introduces Credit Cards Into The UK

Alcatraz federal penitentiary known as "The Rock" closes.

Berlin Wall Opened For 1 Day Passes.

1st Beeching Report suggests closing 25% of British Rail.

Pope John XXIII dies.

Pope Paul VI is elected by College of Cardinals.

The Great Train Robbery takes place in Buckinghamshire, England.

Martin Luther King, Jr. delivers his "I have a dream" speech.

Popular Films - Cleopatra, The Longest Day, Lawrence of Arabia.

Popular TV Programmes - Coronation Street, The Andy Griffith Show, The Flintstones, Mister Ed, The Avengers, The Dick Van Dyke Show.

www.ingramcontent.com/pod-product-compliance
Lightning Source LLC
Chambersburg PA
CBHW060222290526
45789CB00003B/1373